I am Buddhist

Cath Senker
Photography by Jenny Matthews

W

FRANKLIN WATTS
LONDON • SYDNEY

This edition 2010

Franklin Watts
338 Euston Road
London
NW1 3BH

Franklin Watts Australia
Level 17/207 Kent Street
Sydney NSW 2000

Acknowledgements
The author and publisher would like to thank the following for all their help
in the production of this book: Jeff, Joanne, Dillan, Rufus and Aphra
Saunders; Fred and Florence Grumitt, Imogen Majsai, David and Peggy
Williams, and the staff of the Dharma School, Brighton.

The photographs on pages 24-27 were kindly provided by
the Saunders family.

Photographer Jenny Matthews
Designer Steve Prosser
Series editor Adrian Cole
Art director Jonathan Hair
Consultant The Clear Vision Trust

ISBN 978 0 7496 9656 6

A CIP catalogue record for this book is available from the British Library.

Printed in China

Franklin Watts is a division of Hachette Children's Books,
an Hachette UK company.
www.hachette.co.uk

Contents

All about me

My name is Dillan and I'm 8 years old. I live in Brighton. I go to the **Dharma** School, which is the only Buddhist school in Europe.

My favourite activities at school are reading and art.

Outside school
I love writing
stories, playing
games and
climbing trees.

My family

I live with my Mum, Dad, my brother Rufus and my sister Aphra. Rufus is 6 and Aphra is 3. I also have an older brother and sister.

'For us, being Buddhist is about being kind and generous in our daily lives, rather than taking part in special customs.' Dillan's Mum

Mum looks after us and she works as a hairdresser, too. Dad runs a building company.

Nannie and Poppie (my grandparents) live nearby.

My Dad and Uncle Rod work together.

My Buddhist beliefs

To me, the most important thing is to be kind to all living things. If we are careful about what we say, and try not to be hurtful or greedy, everyone will be happier.

I look after living things, like this pumpkin plant, but I know it will die one day.

I try to be gentle towards living creatures. We don't have any pets because I think animals should be free.

I try to stop people hurting each other.

'Buddhism teaches us that everything changes. We can't cling to the past.' Dillan's Dad

Our food

I'm a vegan. I don't eat any products that come from animals. To me, eggs are baby birds. So I don't want to eat them.

I think people should decide for themselves what is right for them to eat.

My favourite foods are porridge, tahini (sesame seed paste), dhal (lentil sauce), pasta, fruit and vegetables.

We put out nuts for the birds, but sometimes the squirrels eat them!

Worship at home

Our family **shrine** has an image of the Buddha. The Buddha is not a god, but a man who lived 2,500 years ago.

Sometimes I offer flowers to the Buddha and light **incense**. The flowers on the shrine wilt and die. This shows how things change. We replace them with new offerings.

Sometimes I sit near the shrine to be peaceful.

Meditation

Some days I find **meditation** easy and other days I don't. I meditate by breathing slowly. It helps me to relax and become calm.

Each day at school we meditate for a short time together.

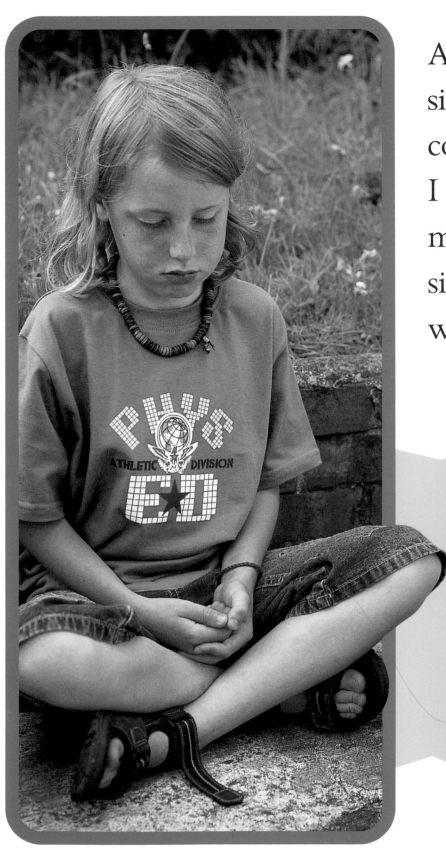

At home I often sit quietly in a comfortable place. I try to 'be in the moment' - just sitting calmly with my thoughts.

You don't have to sit cross-legged to meditate. You just need to be comfortable.

Worship at school

We have **puja** (worship) every day at school. We light a candle and incense. My teacher Imogen reads a story. Her stories always have a message, which is often about friendship.

The incense reminds us to spread loving thoughts in the way that the sweet smell of incense spreads.

Sometimes we sing Buddhist songs, such as 'The Bodhi Tree'. Then we do some chanting and a little meditation.

We learn the hand movements (mudras) that go with the chants.

Learning about Buddhism

At school we learn the same things as other children. Imogen also teaches us about Buddhism. We learn to be thoughtful.

We did a topic on pirates at school.

Our families also learn about Buddhism at the school. They come for puja every Friday.

At school we all help to keep the garden tidy.

Sometimes Buddhist monks visit to talk to us and we share food with them.

Buddhist books

Lots of books explain the Buddha's teachings.
Imogen tells us Buddhist stories.

Imogen is kind. She doesn't shout at
people, even when they're naughty.

Imogen rings the bell to get our attention so that we listen well.

Imogen told us a story about a wise fish. During a drought the other animals fought for water. But the wise fish didn't fight. He called for rain to pour down on everyone. Imogen says we can be like the wise fish and help all living things.

The sangha

Our **sangha**, the Buddhist community, is based around my school. We hold events like this school fair.

All the families get together to feel part of the community. Other people are welcome too. We have storytelling sessions to raise money for the school.

My favourite festival

Kathina is an autumn festival. It thanks
Buddhist monks and nuns. We decorate
our school with autumn leaves and
sing songs to welcome the harvest.

In East Asian countries, people give the monks new robes. We have a visit from monks who live in Chithurst, Sussex. We offer them food, which is called **dana**, and share a meal with them.

The Chithurst monks come to worship with us at Kathina.

Glossary

Bodhi Tree, the
The Buddha was meditating under this tree in India when he realized the truth about life.

chanting
Blessings sung slowly again and again.

dana
An act of generosity or giving.

Dharma
The truth. It also means the teachings of the Buddha.

incense
A stick that gives off a nice smell when it is burned.

meditation
Sitting quietly and breathing slowly to help you become calmer and wiser.

offerings
Gifts such as food or flowers. People place them in front of an image of the Buddha to thank him for his teachings.

puja
Worship.

robes
Long, simple clothes that monks and nuns wear.

sangha
The group of people who follow the teachings of the Buddha.

shrine
A place where people worship. There is usually an image of the Buddha.

Websites

BBC Buddhism website
**www.bbc.co.uk/religion/reli
gions/buddhism/index.shtml**
Information on Buddhist
history, beliefs, customs,
worship and holy days, and
Buddhism in the UK.

Buddhist Studies for Primary
and Secondary Students
**www.buddhanet.net/
e-learning/buddhism/
index.htm**
The primary section includes
guided meditations with
instructions, over 90 stories
about the Buddha, Buddhist
songs and teaching resources.

The Clear Vision Trust
www.clear-vision.org
Details of educational
resources for schools to buy,
including video packs,
artefacts, posters and books.

Dharma for Kids
www.dharmaforkids.com
A Mahayana Buddhist
resource. Includes stories from
the Buddha's life, information
about the Buddhist way of life
and beliefs, and interviews
with monks and nuns.

The Friends of the Western
Buddhist Order
www.fwbo.org
Information about the Buddha
and his teachings, meditation,
the Buddhist festivals, and this
Western Buddhist group.

Note to parents and teachers
Every effort has been made by the Publishers
to ensure that these websites are suitable for
children; that they are of the highest
educational value, and that they contain no
inappropriate or offensive material. However,
because of the nature of the Internet, it is
impossible to guarantee that the contents of
these sites will not be altered. We strongly
advise that Internet access is supervised by a
responsible adult.

Index